The Frontline Collection

Edited by Rufus Mufasa

Published by Iconau
Northcliff
Ferryside
SA17 5RS
www.iconau.com

First published in 2022
© the authors
All rights reserved

ISBN 978-1-907476-36-5

edited by Rufus Mufasa
with Donna Lee-Lewis
typeset in calibri by iconau.com
printed and bound by proprint-wales.co.uk
cover image *motherhood*: a sculpture by Lynne Bebb
design Dominic Williams

Working with Plant Dewi, supported by People Speak Up, this is an exciting anthology that not only captures some of the most neglected superheroes of the pandemic, but it also honours and celebrates motherhood and ramps up resilience, through creativity and empowerment. It allows mothers to testify to the times, for their voices and stories to be honoured, elevated and take up space in language and literature.

The publisher gratefully acknowledges the financial support of Literature Wales and the Royal College of Psychiatrists.

Contents

We Need to Talk

Prelude

I surfed those pandemic waves with that invaluable bootcamp training the winter before the global storm gave me. I ran my creative empire from my tropical bird wallpaper cave, deadlines were the backbone of my diet & flowers were my five a day. Make up was warpaint, Bugzy Malone my soundtrack resurrecting Jemima Nicholas, questioned feminism, faith & fury, studied my eyes blind & sang with the birds. My excitement was intoxicating & my abilities abnormal, I promised the world before the crash came in August 2021, breaking my surfboard leaving me stranded in wild seas.

The crash saved me from cracking wide open but it all slowed me down to a catch up crawl that has delayed this project, a project so important, honouring the female experiences that navigated the pandemic & the emotional backbone of our women.

This collection of voices calls out so much while also celebrating strong women & the many ways they have shaped us & held space for entire families. These voices are honest & generous, important & empowering. These words have held me & we hope they hold you.

In conjunction with the Royal College of Psychiatrists & Literature Wales I ran sessions with young mothers and Plant Dewi. Plant Dewi is located near where I grew up. I had underestimated how much returning to the area would stir up so many emotions.

Because of my adrenaline & in the trenches of sheer unknowing, applications for funding were my new normality.

But my privilege meant that I had to make noise for the realities of the communities I was supporting, with the normality & need for food banks, having to choose between nappies and other essentials, worlds far removed from the people making decisions & calling shots.

I also teamed up with People Speak Up, who pioneered the wellbeing of artists & developed first class hybrid ways of keeping communities connected, trouble shooting absolutely everything, making sure that nobody was left behind. These people became family. Our words reconnected us to self & we danced with our ancestors. This anthology is a celebration of our journey and testament to the power of arts for wellbeing. I remind us all of how this started... my wish for the wellbeing of our mothers, fairer conditions, rights & respect. Future generations depend upon this. The home is our first institution. Our mothers are our world. Women deserve better. Let's take up space, let's sing our song. Joining our choir & peaceful protest are poets from all over Wales & our international collaborative cousins. From Llanelli to Zimbabwe, from Wrexham to India.

I couldn't have completed this without Dominic Williams. I am grateful for his kindness & patience. He is responsible for many great things, both in Wales & Europe. I also need to thank Donna Lee-Lewis for being my eyes when mine were too heavy. Eleanor Shaw wouldn't let this slip & I hope the collection highlights the powerful work that she is pioneering, because this is best-practice in print, this is what social prescribing looks like, this is storytelling that gives us insight & understanding, so that we make our stories better.

Rufus Mufasa

Resilience

Voices of the West

Voices
Offer, -
Ideas,
Companions,
Exchanging
Stories,

Overviewing
Friends,

Tying
Handshakes
Eternally.

Wonderful?
Everlasting
Speaking!!
Timely . . .

Mothership

We carry focus
We carry getting it done
We carry children on hips
We carry everything plus one.

We carry ten steps ahead, tissues
We carry bills, stress, struggle, constant
We carry organisation & superstition
We carry no time for frustration

We carry forms, school uniforms,
Loose change for raffles
We carry pre-packed pre-loved,
Pre-prepared half hassle.

We carry heartache, for us, for them
For our parents, for those passed
Loved ones come with duty
We carry so much on our backs.

Sun Down, Sun Up

I have a visitor,
A stranger who I know too well,
A weight in my chest.
This octopus -
Black

And it grows,
And it shrinks,
But is never truly gone
No matter the poison used to quell it.

When the sun sets
It is given dominion,
And you can only
Wait
For the sun to come up again.

There it is!
Can you see him there
Behind my eyes?
With one slick tentacle
He cradles my heart.
Possessive.

There the sharp beak is
Scratching at my throat.
I can't breathe
Until dawn has broken.

The morning tide
Washes away the ink

That has settled on my lips,
Dried onto my teeth and tongue
With a metal tang, like blood.

He is the leviathan
Whose every motion sways the world,
And he is the invisible needle
That pricks,
Small enough to fool you into
Thinking he is gone for good.

He is the man in black,
The laughter behind your back.
A shape shifter -
But only when the sun is down.

For I have witnessed him
Bleached into scattered atoms
By solar rays,
I have felt the moment
My soul has come unstuck,
The weight untethered.

And I have felt the light
As it kissed my skin in a dance,
And smiled.
And though I know the night will come again,
So too do I know
That the sun will come up in the morning
If I am alive to see it.

Resilience

is my bird
in the hand.
Now my mother's
voice echoes
in my mind
phrases uttered
family humour
reminded of her scent
her cool hands
on my fiery head.

Memories that
fuel my courage
enable me to withstand
all that has gone
and all that will be.

Standing straight and tall
bending when needed
but never breaking.

Female

Releasing strength to protect that female electric energy.

Mothers shield their cubs from what the world may tell women, say to women, pressure women.

The female fight for stable equality, echoes until complete

Mother earth holds us all as one, no matter who or how one presents

Hidden Depths of a Woman

Which mask are you wearing today?
Which one won't give you away?
Which of the many are you going to don?
How many are there for you to put on?

Mother, daughter, carer, wife
So many you need on your passage through life.
Nurse, advisor and counsellor too
But which one of these, is the real you?

Do you remember being a blank page?
Beneath all the layers (including the sage)
Do you have any idea who you must be?
At the very root, like the base of a tree.

Inside your heart is sparkling & clear
Let it all out when anyone is near
Show your facets, diamond-like shine
Joy, love & kindness; you are you – you are fine!

Positive & negative; the ups and the downs
All take their toll, making the lines & the frowns.
Show them all off, as well as your smile
Let you all out, more than once in a while.

You know who you've been right from the start
You know who you are, 'cause you have a heart.
Don't be afraid to show who you really are
Right at the core – a shining bright star!

It Doesn't Have To Be Physical

I don't remember it being like this when I was a child. I don't remember my parents ever getting really cross with each other. Mum dealt with the housework and the household expenses, Dad 'tipping' his wages up to her each week; getting back pocket money. Sounds crazy, but that was how it was in those days, where I grew up. Never once can I remember my Dad getting mad; certainly not with Mum and me.

My first marriage ended when I found out how many times he'd been unfaithful - long time ago now.

But it's the second marriage that caused me fear. And it's true; aggression doesn't have to be physical. This time I thought I'd found my soul-mate. How wrong could I have been?

Sure, it started alright. I felt like a 16 year old whenever he was around, despite me being 42. He used to turn up suited and booted and standing nervously on the door-step. Life was perfect - I thought.

Things changed quickly once it was too late to take a step back. No, not married to him yet, but in deeply with my emotions. By the time we'd been married for less than two years I discovered he'd a problem with his own emotions. Stress, anxiety, depression - call it what you will. The doctor wouldn't, or couldn't, put a name to it when I asked.

It gradually turned to paranoia. I'd slept with my friend's husband when we went to visit. He knew this because he'd heard a noise upstairs and found a telltale mark on my dressing gown. Actually, the noise was my friend's daughter going to the bathroom and the mark he found on my dressing gown was talcum powder.

It only got worse as the years went by till I was too scared to voice a different option.

The TV news would talk about global warming. No such thing he adamantly maintained.

He'd lose his temper at the smallest thing. I'd misread a map or the tap sprayed water over the edge of the sink, or I happen to be between him and the fridge door when he went to get at the milk, or the boiler wasn't doing what it was supposed to do.

Most holidays, when we did take any, were in cottages or caravans, as he didn't like mixing with people in hotels. I didn't argue. It felt like walking on egg shells in attempts not to annoy him.

But things really got worse when he was on long term sick leave. He'd often stay up till 4am or even later, and then sleep for up to 30 hours at a time once he was in bed. I used to stand at the bedroom door sometimes, and listen just to make sure he was still breathing.

He started to lose job after job and eventually I realised his attitude at home was his attitude at work and his bosses wouldn't stand for it.

Before I had met him he had attempted suicide several times. I hadn't known this at first. Then, not long before our marriage collapsed, I walked out after a particularly bad incident, and when I got home I found he'd made another attempt. He didn't tell me. I had to figure it out. But later he gave me the suicide note he'd written.

I was often in my bed at night wondering if I, too, could pluck up the courage to drive over the edge of a cliff. I thought about this for years, but I reckon it takes a certain courage to kill yourself and I'm not that brave - or not that desperate.

The end came when I asked him to explain something on my computer. He was very good at computers, but he always rushed through explanations and I couldn't keep up. I lost my temper. That made a change, and I left the room slamming the door. Unfortunately, a window was open and a breeze caught and slammed the door shut very loudly.

He came after me, grabbed me by the neck and started yelling. This was not the first time that had happened. The thing I remember most was the look on his face. Wide, staring eyes, dribbling mouth, and his shouting. I said I'd go to the police if he hit me, but that annoyed him even more and his response was to grab me tighter and promise to kill me if I did.

Living for years and years, with someone who feels like he did, gets a bit wearing; especially if there is no one close to talk to about it all.

It had taken 25 years to get to the stage where I picked up my coat and handbag and left, never to return except to collect my things. But on that day the only thing I could think of doing was to seek help from Women's Aid.

Eve's Call - The woman's story in her lifetime

He bangs the door late at night
Is given the best portion of the food
Calls it unpalatable, belittles her culinary skills
Beats her up, complains to the gods
Devours her like a snake does its victims
She focusses on not screaming
To prevent the kid's attention!

In the morning, she sweeps
The partitioned shack
To keep it clean!
Goes to the nearby bungalows
Sweeps some more
Cleans the utensils, collects the money
Prepares again for the evening!
Her children too are hungriest at night!

She studied high tech stuff
Fine arts, does the home
Plans vacation, packs their clothes, buys the tickets
Navigates the taxi!
She is the pilot of the plane, the commander of the ship,
The helping hand in the labour room
Women as we know them
Are all wonder creatures!

Yet, eve's daughters

They are held responsible
For all things ever going wrong!
Wasn't eve the one to tempt Adam
To pluck and taste
The juicy, the red,
The tangy and crispy
Forbidden fruit of the tree of knowledge!
We all got doomed
For she mated with Adam the man!
And produced his children!
The curse continues
The tree of wisdom shook its branches
Shed its leaves, apples glistened , orchard smiled
Heavens cried, Adam and eve were sent to earth and
here they stayed!

The pundits of the Hindu scriptures called the woman
doorways to hell!
She argued, critiqued
Sang and studied
They somewhat relented and agreed, motherhood
Was a holy office!

The fight continues
Said the beloved
It's love, no shame
And look my friends
We finally got a day to honour, love's sweet face!

Make the outdoors safe again

Don't stay out late they said
Don't wear short clothes they said
Not even tight, loosen up
But always be on your guards they said
They said all of this to girls alone
Big and small, growing and grown
In towns across the world
Why didn't they ever tell the men
To never abuse! To make the outdoors safe again!

My Body

I take you by the hand
lead you across this abandoned asylum that is my body.

I show you in a private room the tea stain birth marks the
size of your thumb.

Here, you've just got to see the purple dead mountains
of my kneecaps.
I was riding down a hill four years old when a stone the
size of a boulder stood in my way.
I slammed on the breaks and the bike under me stopped
but I kept on going.
Winded mid-air by handlebars too small for my growing
hands.
I learnt then that no brake pads could slow me down, no
matter what stopped in my way
That I couldn't stop before every boulder in my path.

As the stone turned into a diamond in the sunlight
spinning in the air next to me.
I learnt that the grass ahead was always a little out of
reach.
That sometimes the sweetest taste is gravel on your
tongue.

I move the back of your hands up my thigh
Feel the eyes of a horned girl in your knuckles.
Tattoo's so I can sleep with art galleries.
Ram skull illusion.
I can rebuild the ashes of a funeral pyre

It's here I have to slow down.
Where the audio tour needs a leap of faith.

Not used to decoding the fire between my legs.
I was 20 before I smoked the kindling
Or sang hymns to myself by the campfire.

We keep going.

Heartbeat skip
shame
where you cross the silver stretch-mark ocean
deepest fears. My anxieties
build a bridge between me and you.

I have a fox to guide me through the forest.
A vixen of screams haunted night.
Two winged magpies sketched across a broken ribcage
searching of the silver in other people's eyes.

One for sorrow. Two for joy.
Three for a girl and four for a boy.

Flowers in full bloom forever from my hips.
Under this pale frame skin my lungs breath in the
essence of you.

Here, too many eyes seen
names spill from jugs of milk.
Sit balanced on collar bone scaffolding.

I'll hold your wrist across my lips to kiss your heartbeat.
Mimic the throbbing of my head that make sense of a

world we created
where this, is other than you.

The red skin of the heal of your palm.
Scar tissue
lifeline
follow the vein
to the pauses.

Here, I took a needle and sewed happiness into my skin
with no thread; with red thread.
Here, freckles blossom like winter flowers

In one hand the knife held to my own throat.
In the other a quill made from phoenix feathers.

The Cartographer Remarks

Slowly,
my body idles into conversation.

And I sit;
as a cartographer to the land of self-deprecation,
jotting down the changes in landscape.

The equator is much wider now,
The smile ripples to the shore

The breasts are so much closer to the tide
and the gap is almost indiscernible
between these two tectonic plates
I call my thighs.

A carcophy of native voices
Note my collection of chins,
Skims over the curvature of
My-numb-mum-tum
As gravity pulls my spine into a question mark.

And the secret garden?
Is now a shrine to overgrown topiary.

I can't remember the last time I mowed my legs.
As my son palms the sand dunes of my cheeks.

My mum weaves pyjamas in bigger sizes that I squeeze
into my nightstand.

The cartographer notes the way my bingo wings flutter in
the breeze.
The roast-ham cross-hatch of my breast feeding bras.

On the whole, the land is looking newborn tired.

See, my pre-pregnancy body was a map along the
well-trodden dirt-track of my childhood, like here;
When my Grandma took my stabilisers, it was the closest
I'd ever be to flying.

Unravelling into early-morning coffee stains and easy
mistakes.
I'd pour over the details between vodka shots and cheap
cigarettes.

But my pregnant body brough the incessant conversation
of the cartographer to her knees.
Just a portrait of me,
Sitting at the edge of the bathwater
Waiting for the line to turn blue.

At playgroups,
In a bar
The cartographer recounts how it feels to fall out of love
with stretch marks,
How every touch is thaw to a frozen lake.

Or how we are all looking back at a map we knew once,
When the pool was fresh ink and warm water.

My body waltzes into conversation
So I ask her:
'Why take coal, and turn it into diamonds
just to burn it anyway?'

The River

Mother, come by the river to pray.
Sister, come by the river to pray.

Pull damp rag
crimson tide
from your teething jaw//raw
and bathe.

Feel the water raise//rise.
It is purer after you pray.

Hand-to-knee
feel the rip of earth
clot//clod at the roots of weeds
 and push//pull.

The river will erode/
/corrode the limitations of its banks and return the land to
sea.

The illusional stability of land will cease,
built upon chalk-drawn dawn
against a dark cavern face.

Illuminated only by lamplight//moon-night.

The river cuts down the façade of rock to view its self-
portrait.

The river, as a lover
Breaks the confines of its frame to accommodate harmony
with the breeze.

Women, come by the river to pray.
See the true reflection of sisters in the time//sand.
Loosen the lead weight//noose//tension beneath your
child

and pray

Burrnesha (or the last Sworn Virgin)

One gesture and on the ground falls the skirt
final vestige of your womanhood.
A defiant braid surrenders at your feet
with proud copper reflections.
Your breast is unripe. You touch
the pomegranate skin and
you bind it up. Two cruel bandages
constraining the breath. Folded is the bridal veil
that once was your mother's (a dream
of apple and cinnamon guarded by camphor).
A fragment of glass reflects
your trembling face. On the bed
ragged pants are waiting
for your milky skin. Far away a chorus
of voices and laments. Your father
is resting in the largest room.
Barely an amaranth scarf

hides the blossom of blood
memento of wild hunting.
You're alone to keep the honor of home,
family and county. Tomorrow
facing the elderly
with eyes of ice
you'll deny being a woman.
It's a fight, a trade for your freedom.
Smoky cellars of raki and sweat
are waiting for you. Your belly is barren forever.
The law of mountains and valleys, of impetuous
hastening rivers
is written in blood since remote times
- Alone, a Virgin, is worth only six oxen -
Tomorrow, you'll be a man. For love a hand
sighs and torments
when the Moon is not looking.

Burrnesha (ovvero l'ultima vergine giurata)

Un sol gesto ed è in terra la veste
reliquia di donna. S'arrende
ai tuoi piedi la treccia ribelle
di fieri riflessi di rame.
Acerbo il tuo seno. Ne sfiori
la pelle color melograno e
lo avvolgi. Due bende crudeli
costringono il fiato. Piegato il velo
da sposa che fu di tua madre, già sogno
di mela e cannella custodito da canfora.
Un frammento di vetro riflette
le gote tremanti sul letto
calzoni consunti in attesa
di pelle di latte. Lontano un coro
di voci e lamenti. Tuo padre
è composto nella stanza più grande.
A stento una sciarpa amaranto

nasconde quel fiore di grumi di sangue
memento di caccia selvaggia.
Sei sola a serbare l'onore di casa,
famiglia e contado. Domani
di fronte agli anziani
con occhi di ghiaccio
negherai d'esser donna.
È una lotta, un baratto per la tua libertà.
Cantine fumose di raki e sudore
ti aspettano con ventre per sempre infecondo.
La legge di valli montane e fiumi impetuosi
è scritta nel sangue da tempi remoti
-una vergine sola vale solo sei buoi.-
Domani sei uomo. Per l'amore una mano
sospiri e tormenti nel letto
da sola.

Womanhood and Me

To me true womanhood is being part of a tribe
A place that feels like home, safe and secure
Somewhere you can be completely yourself
Where you are accepted and empowered
You know that your back is protected
And you have their back no matter what

Shared stories, emotions and rituals
Your words are truly heard
And your voice is important
Being part of something bigger than yourself
Wisdom and knowledge is handed down
I can feel fire in my spirit
Water in my blood
Air in my breath
Mother nature in my soul
And Earth holding my body

I feel alive and free
Imperfections are welcomed and embraced
There is no hierarchy
We are all equal and respected
Love is unconditional
Alone time is refreshing and encouraged
Guilt free healing and self-care
Women are celebrated
Sacred and pure flow of your own unique energy

Living with the cycles of nature
Where there is no greed
Where there is enough for everyone
We are seen as human beings, not human doings
And there is no such thing as a women's role
Chores are exactly that, just chores
We are capable of anything
With the right to choose
The life that suits us best
No power or cohesive threat
Just live and reach your full potential
Plenty of joy, fun and peace
Laughs galore and tears true
A spoken truth from heart to heart
Now is the time, so lets make the start

Salute

A Visit from Mammy underneath the Garden Oak (Mum in spirit world since 2008).

CWTCH up closer to the tree Louise.
Don't reach for the branch, as the branch is happy to reach you.
Accept this kind embrace from the branch of truth, in recognition of your own.

Reach out more selectively Cariad, and let others be awakened and given the final chance to deliver.

Remember Lulus my words of "Now fuck off my dear", and use-use-use, my wise but common essence of words, oh so naughty but creates laughter for the not guilty ones, but squirms from the insincere ones, needing to be told. Keep it up until your message lands loud, or silent clear tone with usage of words that hits the bullseye, and a mark forever present. Leave no doubt that your mission isn't silence!

Wiser reaching out needed Lulus, and time people woke up and delivered. Your lockdown multifaceted due to lots of serious crap-SHIT caused by the hands of unscrupulous people, but let's turn shit to manure for nourishing the now new growth. Go for it Lulus, you show them!

Your lockdown not new-took force in 1992!

Yes people, stop and think.

Lockdowns of multifaceted origins so true for the forgotten minority since time began. NOT GOOD ENOUGH PEOPLE! So many needless voices of the minority lost to stubborn still walls and closed doors.

Thanks to Covid19 or people not listening, so much needless suffering, or essential and perfect experiences if soul deep spirited perspective believed.

The pandemic enforced lockdown on the masses - for a moment the majority might have a window of understanding.

Now the minority are experts in this domain. We have strategy and tools.

Lulus do your stuff, and sod the silence!
BIG BIRD SPREADS HER WINGS.
IN FLIGHT FOREVER FREE!

Caru chi Mammy - fy ffydd bob dydd

Mam

Everyone called her mam, so naturally I did too. This tiny woman always dressed in the same clothes – black skirt down to her boots; black blouse – high necked collar; cameo; pinny; hair in a bun and spectacles that sat permanently on the end of her nose.

Because my mother, her sister and three brothers especially had been rather a wayward lot in their youth, mam ruled at home... not with an iron bar perhaps but a hefty rolling pin. They all lived in awe of their mother and dare not disobey. What mam said was law. By the time I was old enough to realise this, the boys, my uncles, were in the army, while my mother – having been abandoned by her husband - was employed in the munitions factory with her sister.

As I said I also called her mam – although in fact we were not related – not by blood anyway. My mother, her eldest daughter, had adopted me as a baby. When the marriage fell apart it was left to mam to raise me. Mam, having been left to bring up five children on her own after the death of her husband in a mining accident, reckoned another child made no difference.

To me my mam was wonderful. Although kind, in her no nonsense way, there were few hugs and kisses, yet she radiated love. Somehow, despite food being rationed and in short supply, there was always something to eat. She kept me by her side as she did her chores, teaching me how to bake and roll out pastry. She taught me to sew and embroider. She had this wonderful sewing box full of buttons, ribbons, silk thread. There were pretty bits of material cut from discarded clothes and cardboard cut-out templates used for making quilts. As we sat by the fire on a cold winter evening, stitching or knitting, while bloaters (herrings) spat and sizzled on the hearth for our supper, I never doubted that everyone had a mam like mine.

She had rules and sayings that everyone had to abide by – no gambling, alcohol or card playing indoors – and no swearing. The colourful chalk ornaments won at the local fair, she'd consider unlucky. They were duly smashed and buried in the garden. However, when there was boxing on the radio mam would be there, ear pressed to the wireless, fists clenched, shouting advice and criticism. American, Sugar Ray Robinson was her favourite. Mam expected women to mind their Ps and Qs. Dare a female whistle in her presence, she'd show her displeasure by declaring – 'A whistling woman and a crowing hen are neither fit for God nor men.'

I never did learn how to whistle.

Mum

She had vascular dementia. I watched as day by day she diminished. Yet she stood straight and could be nimble at times especially when something prompted her to dance. She was stick thin towards the end and she had few words except to say she wanted to die. Her beautiful brown eyes had sunk into her head and her once glorious auburn hair had paled to sand. Her sensuous lips were captured in a perpetual pout of despair, fear, confusion at the increasingly incomprehensible world that surrounded her. But this poor ghost was not the mother I knew.

My father called her his 'little red hen' but there was nothing fluffy about her. She was beautiful, slim, forceful, fierce even and she loved to dance. All this despite a shaky start in life. Her father left when she was nine and she recalled leaping on his back to stop him beating her sweet, gentle mother. For most of my life I thought him dead. But he had his own demons to deal with. His father was imprisoned twice for child neglect of him and his sister. They were found without food or warmth left for days on end but unlike him my mother was fiercely protective and did her best for my sister and I. She made us believe that we could be anything we wanted to be.

Mum met and married my Dad when the war drew to a close. He was kind and loving and smart as a tack. He adored her. She was his one and only though she could be difficult at times. The four of us lived in a two up, two down with my nanny and great grandmother, a house full of women but dad could take it. The house was red-bricked and old, dirty, damp, cramped, a slum really, just yards off the busy New Chester Road opposite Camel Lairds Shipyard in Rockferry. Mum was like an exotic bird, trapped and restless, struggling to keep us all clean and safe until one day she broke.

I don't know what the final straw was. Maybe the washing line snapped and trailed our clean clothes in the coal dust that coated the back yard. Maybe my sister or I toddled toward the thundering traffic at the end of our street. Maybe we visited the lovely new house her best friend has just moved into. I don't know, but she took herself down to the council offices and refused to budge until we were rehoused.

What went through her mind as she approached the imposing Georgian splendour of Hamilton Square? Only hope and a fierce determination could have sustained her as she faced the grey-suited officials and demanded to be rehoused. I wonder what they made of this lovely woman and her lonely protest? Did she cry? Did she shout? Did she plead? What ever it was, she succeeded. Shortly after, we moved into a three bedroomed house on a new council estate. We had an indoor bathroom and a garden and there was grass everywhere. I was only five but I still remember our excitement.

Mum left school when she was only thirteen and I often wonder what she could have achieved with her strength of character and her courage. She was loving but her criticisms could sting and our relationship was sometimes strained. Nevertheless, I always knew she had my back and would support me no matter what. She was Mum, My Mum.

A Special Bond

'You're so like your grandmother,' my mother would sometimes say. I'd never given it much thought until recently. Lockdown, and days spent alone, found me looking through old photograph albums and pondering about my family.

I had a special bond with my paternal grandmother. Born from my grandparent's home in Weymouth, my early years were spent living there with my parents. Dad was the youngest of three sons and his brothers had both produced boys, so when I arrived Nana was literally over the moon.

This idyllic life changed when Dad's job, as an electronics engineer, took us east to Lowestoft, to work at Pye Radio.

I missed Nana and Grandan (as I called him), and Whiskers, their beautiful black and white cat. Every week Nana wrote me a postcard. I still have those cards. After starting school, I'd spend the summer holidays with them as by this time I had a baby brother keeping my mother busy. Nana ran a B&B for summer visitors. Helping her with little chores I got to know the regulars. When they were leaving they'd slip me a sixpence, sometimes even a shilling. You could buy a lot of sweets for sixpence!

Some days we'd walk the short distance to the beach and

enjoy an ice-cream. I still love an ice-cream. Or we'd pop down to the little bakers shop at the end of her cul-de-sac to buy an iced bun for tea. I've never tasted an iced-bun as delicious as those.

My earliest memories of Nana were her kind, smiling eyes framed by big round spectacles. Her long, white hair was worn up in a bun. In the evening I would watch as she brushed it out before braiding it into a plait. I yearned to have long hair but my mother wouldn't allow me to grow it. I remember how she never went out without a hat and wore dark colours, and the same style of shoe. These were lace-ups with a medium, solid heel to give her height, and to accommodate her bunions. I have photos of her sitting on a rug on the beach in her felt hat, secured with a long hat-pin.

One day my mother told me Nana and Grandan would be coming to stay with us for a while. The dining room was converted to a bedroom. I can still see that bright, sunny room, painted primrose yellow. A large bay window looked out on the front garden and an enormous cherry blossom tree.

A few weeks before my ninth birthday, I contacted measles. One afternoon I drifted off to sleep with Nana lying on the twin bed beside me, reading a book. Still half-asleep, I found myself crying out: 'Nana's going to die. Nana's going to die'. My mother had rushed in the room, followed by my shocked father, his brother and Grandan. Nana had taken my hand, trying to comfort me. It's a memory that will live with me forever.

I told them how I'd seen Nana floating above the bed, like a cloud, all in white. I had no concept of death or that she was ill with angina. Parents didn't discuss subjects like illness and death with their children.

That evening I kissed Nana goodnight and went upstairs to my own bed. In the early hours of the morning Nana slipped away.

When I go walking on a windy day, I take my hair up into a bun. I look in the mirror at navy trousers and jacket. She loved the colour navy-blue. At night I brush my hair and plait it. I don't like hats but, like Nana, I too love cats. She doted on her younger son, born later in life, as mine was. She loved and spoilt her grandchildren. Yes, we had a special bond.

My Grandma Was Great

One of the most inspiring women I have ever known was my Grandma.

At 16 she ran away from home, due to a wicked step mother, and eventually found her way from Bristol to a huge house in Kent where she became a maid. It was not until many years later that I discovered I lived only 500 yards away from that house.

Her hair was truly amazing. The story goes her wicked step-mother was jealous of my Grandma and the woman cut her long black hair very short. That was the final thing in a long line of incidents which caused Grandma to run away. She never had it cut again and wore it in two long plaits wound around her head like a crown. Out of all her grandchildren I was the only one allowed to brush it.

She was married in 1916 to Arthur after he had been discharged from the army when his right leg was shot off in WW1. They had six children and, although Granddad worked when he could, there were many times Grandma was the only financial support for the family. As there were no social benefits in those days, Grandma did her best to save money. For instance, toothbrushes were loaded with soot from the chimney.

She took in washing, delivered babies, laid out the dead - for which she got paid 6d (2½p). She kept pigs, chickens and ducks and grew food in the back garden. She was a fantastic cook and her pastry was something umm um. Mind you, although her cooking tasted wonderful, I am still wary of a recipe I have of hers for tomato ketchup which contains 2lbs (that's nearly a kilo) of salt!

I lived with her and Granddad when Mum worked; going home at weekends, so the influence she had on my life was profound.

Despite my shame she made sure I went to school in the winter dressed in thick woolly stockings, a vest and a corset (I was around 12 years old at the time). But I did felt smug in that I was the only child at school with a warm, comforting glow in the winter, which came from the glass of her home-made elderberry wine that she gave me each school morning.

She was loving and kind, but stood no nonsense. For instance, one of my cousins had a habit of holding his breath till he turned blue if he was refused anything he thought his by rights. She'd whip down his trousers and underpants and plonk him on the cold marble kitchen worktop, which made him take a deep breath in shock and cure his little tantrum. He eventually learnt.

When there was sickness she was always there, peeling and de-piping grapes, mopping sweaty brows and bathing grazed knees. 'Oh, me little duck, come and give us a cuddle', if one of her grandchildren needed reassurance.

She taught me care of animals, but not over sentimentality when the need for food was paramount – eggs and bacon appeared on the breakfast table and there was no discomfort that a few days before the eggs had been under hens and the bacon had been trotting around the pigsty.

Her legacy to me, I think, is a determination to see things through, even when times get tough. So thank you Edith Veronza Wadsworth.

My WI

I came to Wales in 2007 when retiring from work. My neighbour soon invited me to join the WI and I inquired as to what was the WI. I soon found out. At the first meeting the President asked if I'd enjoyed the meeting. 'They're awfully noisy', was my reply. But they forgave me and, since then I've made amazing and loving friends.

Who knew I'd go fly fishing. I felt guilty about this as I don't approve of 'blood' sports, but the casting action is supposed to be good for the arm muscles after a mastectomy. It didn't occur to me till much later that it was my right arm I was casting with, but the mastectomy had been of my left breast!

I've appeared on YouTube in Bryn WI Operation Teacake to celebrate our 50th anniversary – we're still there if you wish to look us up.

Played parts such as a mouse in *The Owl and the Pussy Cat*, been one of Rebecca's daughters, Buttons in a panto and sang *Hen Wlad Fy Nhadau* at the WI's AGM 100th anniversary in the Royal Albert Hall and much, much more.

But it is the sisterhood which makes our WI so amazing.

Both times I had breast cancer they were there for me. Supportive and caring. Even to the point where one member arranged for the Hwyl Girls Choir to come and sing outside my door one Christmas.

And when my marriage ended one of my 'sisters' came to help paint my new flat, whilst others moved me in and even donated much needed furniture and kitchen equipment.

One even bought me some pickled walnuts when I said I'd never heard of them before - they're very tasty.

There is neither the time nor the space here to tell all of the 14 years of sisterhood I've been privileged to share with my lovely WI ladies.

Journey to the Centre

Above and above the reed-ringed lake
Of blue flat tranquil water spread below,
I find this confusion of mounds:
Does the ground slope up or down?
Trees seem more massive than is possible,
Sunlight fragmented, from all parts
Of the sky at once, swung and spinning.
A narrow passageway inwards between the rocks,
Beset by bushes set in mossed earth
And a muted twilight of worn silver-green...
Then I am face to face with Her.
My wrist is fastened by the grip of Her hand.

I am once again where I began,
Among white birches in mild sunlight;
I walk out of the trees; an autumn day
On which I see my mother some way off,
Carrying her warm-held baby home.
The baby girl who is myself, dreaming;
And as I walk from the trees, she dreams
Of me emerging from the forest,
Just as I go onwards to the house
To step into her dream and then become
That child who is myself, the mind
And self who must travel the length
Of my life, across six decades...
Yet this time the wind rises,

Sweeping me back beyond the birches,
Into the great space ocean, limitless,
Where there is only Her bright voice,
Speaking from behind the wind.
She lifts me, sets me back in the climates
Of the world; seas, mouths of rivers, beaches, cliffs.
I am a floating awareness, outward-directed,
Without mass or substance or self or sadness,
Watching, an awareness only, looking outward on the
world,
A smile within Her smile.

The Nurturing of a Personality
Who I am – what am I, Margaret Hannah Davies, a mixed product of the influential people in my life.
Born in Gorseinon, a demanding 10 1/2 lb. human being to be nurtured and cared for.

My Mother
My Mother was a proud caring lady, very strict, must be obeyed, and my father and I knew it. Where I went, who I played with, what I wore, yes that was how it was, and she was right. She had beautiful pale blue eyes, thick hair which went white at an early age, dyed it with Henna colour and lovely skin:

She was 10 years younger than my father. Refused to marry until WW1 was over when she was 29. She was very much a home maker, cooking every day. Monday was Corn Beef day, Tuesday washing day, Wednesday Lamb Chops day, and my favourite was Saturday when she cooked the meat joint, cabbage and rice pudding, which my father and I enjoyed every Saturday night after my bath time.

When I would pout I would sit on the cold front door step. She would say "You'll have piles sitting there, what do you want?" to which I replied "A kiss friends" and that was sufficient for me to have my own way.

Her world was her family next door and my father and me. Not a socialiser at all. Every November I hear her telling me "What about making the Christmas puddings?"

She lived to 92 years old, still the boss. Lived with us for 6 years, still having her hair coloured brown. Still in charge although physically unable to move easily, but mentally alert. Even in my teenage years I had to be home by 9:30pm. I would run up the road although there would be trouble if I was late. What trouble I never found out. She spoke Welsh to my Father and English to me.

My Grandmother (Mamgu)

My maternal Grandmother lived next door. Having brought up 6 children she fostered her little niece Mary Anne Pugh and also her grandson 18 months old to help her eldest daughter Sarah Anne cope with her newly born baby. Rather Victorian in her dressing. Her favourite saying was "Lle i popeth a popeth yn ei le". A place for everything and everything in its place. Yes, I remember, try to do so but with so many files, books and hobbies in my life I emphasise "I try Mamgu".

Her maiden name was Margaret EVANS, married William DAVIES, called Marged. My mother nee Margaret DAVIES married John EVANS, called Maggie. I was Margaret EVANS (everyone was forbidden to call me anything but Margaret) and yes providence saw that I married Wallace DAVIES, and so we had Evans to Davies, Davies to Evans and Evans to Davies. Two sons and five grandsons that was it.

Mamgu spent the last two years of her life with us and passed away when I was 15 years old.

Auntie Lou

Then there was my Auntie Louise who I called Auntie Lou. A career woman, very proud. She taught me to sew, starting with dolls cothes. Later on in life her advice was "If you have a shilling out it somewhere to make it two.

If you spend one you will still have one. Spend the first and you will have nothing." And "Don't have anything you cannot afford and keep away from money lenders".

A very pretty lady who dressed well. I spent the whole of my August holidays in Llanelli with her. I was fortunate in that it was like I had two mothers. She married a lovely man Uncle Frank. When she was 39 he died after 4 years of marriage.

I would go away with her on holidays to London, Llandrindod and Aberystwyth. Sadly she is the only one in my family that had Dementia, always remembering me and my family who she relied on and she was 91 years old when she passed away.

My Gregg's Teachers

I am also grateful to my teachers at Gregg's Business College, Swansea who gave me confidence which is what I lacked in my earlier days. I was happy at Gregg's for two years from 14 to 16 years of age. They made me realise that I could be successful at subjects I learned to love. I danced Continental Tango in my lunch break. Now in my 92nd year I look back at the benefits I have had throughout my life by listening and following their examples, who cared enough to teach me to cook, sew, handle money, gave me a Christian faith and conversed in Welsh as my Grandparents were unfamiliar with the English language.

A tan will fade but memories last forever.

We Need to Talk

The Big DDDDDDDDDDDDDD

On no, here we go again, Remember ME
You thought I'd gone, BUTTTTTTT
I wont let you forget me.
My name is Dee, I rhyme with tree.
Now sit on the sofa, stare at the TV
Your home is your haven, as safe as can be
Eat some cake, much easier than following a recipe
Sleep all day, awake all night, try to grab a little cat nap
Wrap your cocoon, oh so tight, squeeze your body
sensations out wide.
Forget all the crap, this will soon end
Ignore your phone, ignore your friends
Who is that imposter inside your head?
Is it the devil or is it your friend?
Hide from your family and just pretend
That you are ok, that time again
Where there is chaos, there's light to transcend
To beat the sorrow, till I visit again.

Now take your tablets, do what your told
There is no medal, there is no gold.
One step at a time is all it takes
Do what you feel like, don't do what you hate
Just ride the moment like the eye of the storm
Now I am leaving, turn that frown upside down
But I will be back as you well know.

Motherhood is a Trigger

Motherhood is a trigger
I feel the trauma of my mother and hers
I am an overflow
And I overflow
I fear for my daughters
Because they are daughters
And not sons

Mary Ann was 40 when she had my grandmother
She was long done having children, her boys were grown
and gone

And then there was Elaine, my Mams
At 17 she met a boy (Harry, his name was)
She would dance with him at the Ritz
Her first love

Elaine and Harry went to Mary Ann
And said they needed to get married
Needed to
Mary Ann knew what this meant
She sent Harry home
Called home her sons
Who took Elaine out into the street and beat her blue
Because it was more important to show the neighbours
They were prideful
Than it was to love her

Harry's parents said no, he had a future to think about
A life to live
My grandmother was devastated, disgraced
They sent her away, pregnant, scared
To a nun-run mother and baby home
Where the newly pregnant scrubbed the floors
And the heavily pregnant waited for the day they would
become mothers
But only for a moment

Harry died – a heart condition
He was only a boy
He never got a chance to live the life

There is a photo of my mams at his funeral
They let her come back for a moment
A fresh grave
Overflowing with flowers
Dressed in a wide black coat
To hide her growing belly

My auntie Debbie was born
My grandmother never told me the story of that night
I never got the chance to ask

They kept her at the home for months
Because she said
'No, you're not taking my baby
No.'

Mary Ann wouldn't let her come home
Until my auntie was 18 months old
She scraped by
But you can see from the pictures that
something in her eyes had died

A couple of years later she met my grandfather
Ronnie his name was
I can't remember him, he died when I was 4 months old
He married her after a few weeks
(She wouldn't do it otherwise)
They had 4 kids

She told me she knew straight away
She told me he was the only one for her
True love

Ronnie
My mother told me he was one for a drink
Spent his pay every Friday in the Workies
And my grandmother had to get a job
Scrubbing floors and watching the babies
Of the rich
To pay the rent
Scraped up the kids with what she could manage

Ronnie
My mother told me he was one with his fists
Broke my grandmother's nose, her ribs

My mother told me
'She would pack up her bags and say she was going
Every time
But she would always stay'

One day my grandmother said 'Come on, we're going'
Gathered up her things, her kids
But my mother said
'No. Don't pretend. You're not going, not really.
You never do'
And that's when she stopped believing

Ronnie died young, bloated from the cancer
The men went to the funeral
And the women stayed at home
Like they were supposed to
My mother told me it was the drink that did it
My grandmother
Never looked at another man again

When I was little I asked how he died
My cousin Ray told me that he was
Frightened to death by the severed claws of a bear
I like that story better

When I was 18 months old my mother had a baby
Her name was Cassandra
Cassy
2 months later my mother woke up in the morning

And Cassy was dead, cold in the crib
It was 4 days before Christmas
They buried her in the same grave as Ronnie
The dirt hadn't even settled

My mother doesn't talk about these things
But sometimes it leaks out as anger when you least
expect it

My grandmother was our world
She had 6 kids, and they had kids
Her house was where we congregated
Headquarters
Breakfast every Saturday,
Chicken dinner for 20,
Victoria sponge for 30
She would send me to Chalkies
With a tenner to buy butter, eggs
And Golden Virginia
She wasn't like my mother, or her mother, not hard
She was sensitive, but weary
And always told you she was proud of you

I was six months pregnant when she died
Lung cancer
A tumor, 9 centimeters long
She hid it for a long time
Once I caught her coughing into a tissue
My eye clocked the blood before she could
Whip it out of sight

Radiotherapy
My mother took her every week
I thought she was getting better
Then one day I called my parents to ask how she was
And my father said 'She's going to die tonight,
Sorry babe'.

My mother, my sister, my aunties, uncles, cousins all
went to the house
But I stayed at home
Paralyzed by fear
Never had I felt such a pain
I tried to stay calm
I didn't want to hurt the baby
And in the morning she was gone
But the daffodils on her window had bloomed

There is no one
To tell me that they're proud now
So I do it for myself

I named my daughter Elaina
After my mams
I look at her pictures
I try to honour her
Knickerbocker glories every birthday
Christmas decorations up just after Halloween

I try to feel my mother's love
Try to feel it even in the slap of her words
She sends me seven kisses in every text
She loves my children fiercely
She is a protector

Live Fear Free

Taking the blows day after day
Over and over, it's not ok
Talk with someone, never stay silent
Horrendous shouting turns to violence

Echo those feelings of breaking free
Remember you can change your destiny
Carry on believing, it won't take long
Remember your shine, keep your song strong

Menopause and Mojo

Oh no mojo, not again! Where have you gone?
One minute you're here with me, the next you've moved
on.

The mood swings come, both up and down
One minute there's a smile and the next there's a frown.

The slightest things affect me – so sensitive I can be
Crying at silly films or even someone felling a tree!

My coping mechanisms have diminished at such a speedy
pace
And organisational skills gone up the spout - I'm so not
on the case.

My body temperature gauge has really thrown a wobbly
Hot flushes, night sweats abound and sometimes my
skin's kind of knobbly!

My sleep patterns are hugely disrupted and that's just
another thing
From sleeping like a baby or log and then hearing
everything.

Eating like the proverbial pig. Yes – that's everything in
sight
No diets work nor dry months – forget any food that's
light!

Our body shape transitions – an extra stomach now appears
And I'm really not going to comment about our thighs, our hips and rears.

Yet, still we seem to manage, to push right on through life
Even though inside we scream and want to stab someone with a knife.

I also feel sorry for our men who never can understand
For they can't know what we're going through – to them it's a foreign land.

With all these things we have, we women are still so strong
Periods, babies and then menopause – the list is terribly long.

And yet in other countries, their women don't get the same
So is it beliefs and programming, or is sugar really to blame?

Perhaps if we eat real clean and walk 10,000 steps a day
And meditate each morning, then health with come our way?

So mojo – I ask – where have you gone? I really need you
back.
Without you I have to start over again – without you
there is such a lack.

Mojo – please I beg of you – return – come back right
now
You're so important to me – to stop me being a cow

Mojo – I'm sorry, please forgive me – without you I feel
so blue
I appreciate you oh so much more – thank you and I love
you.

Casy Study A – Del and Steph's Story

STEPH: I am an individual. A while ago, I signed up for story telling sessions, not knowing what I was letting myself in for until I found myself sitting in a circle of people in a room of grey and glass with a black floor. This would be the first time I told my story to anyone. But first, Delyth started to tell hers.

DELYTH: In 2007 I was diagnosed with breast cancer. I called it Bob.

STEPH: To go back in time, to 2010 I had received my usual letter for breast screening at Morrisons. Well, the mobile unit outside that is. So, I went along and thought nothing more about it until I received an appointment for further investigations. The resulting biopsy led to a lumpectomy in Prince Philip's and an appointment in Singleton. There my consent was sought to send samples to America for testing to decide which treatment would be best for me.

The worst time during that period was the waiting - about six or seven weeks – before the results came back. Would I be told I needed chemotherapy or, worst or all, that I had no chance of survival?

When the results were in I sat trying to listen to what I was being told, but all I could concentrate on was the clean smell of the room, the curtains moving gently around the examination couch and the noise of the world going on outside as if all ......was......perfectly normal.

DELYTH:
- Charlotte elbowed me in the chest
- Tenerife holiday
- Came back, saw GP - 15 week waiting list
- Went to see Simon Holt privately, used the Micky Mouse fund
- MRI scan, 500 photos - Bob only showed in one
- 3 weeks later I went for the results on my own in Bancyfelin
- Right side, then let's talk about the left, cancer word was used for the first time
- Life fell apart from the front doors of Bancyfelin to the car, ringing my sister Sian, months to us the cancer word in the same sentence as me.
Nobody knew, I could hide it, still working

STEPH: To hear that I had a 72% chance of still being around in five years' time and that I needed no chemo, only radiotherapy, and a drug to keep things under control — pooh - relief.

My radiotherapy was undertaken at Singleton. At one session I was asked if a trainee radiographer could carry out the procedure. Well, we all have to learn, so I agreed. Turns out he was a young man in his 20's and when he laid his hands on me, I squeaked. He jumped back in horror and it was apparent that he and the rest of the staff, all female, thought I might scream 'sexual misbehaviour'. In fact, I merely wanted to point out that before placing his hands on someone in the middle of November he really should warm them up.

Five years later I found another lump... Sometimes, my mind still takes me back to when I sat at the bus stop outside Prince Philip's hospital shivering and trembling, despite it being in the middle of summer, with knowledge that this time I needed chemotherapy, a complete mastectomy, and yet another type of drug. But again, my treatment was tailor-made.

DELYTH:
- Room with a view...
- Room description- small room, viewing window, seagulls, sea, summer day, children playing, cars back and forth....
- Where you going - voice from the desk by the lift
- Lift 1-2- 5-6-10-11-12 floors
- Outside on the bench - car - go!-go! left then right at the lights
- On my wall, description of my wall, what I can see and smell
- You may know my wall – where
- What I am wearing - fluffy PJS, cannula in hand, slippers and bald head
- Fish and chips and Joe's ice-cream

- Back in the lift - secret world in the lift, smell
- Where have you been - hours gone, couldn't find you
- Back in my room with a view
- Explain Singleton ward 12 - room with a view
- Next time you go down the Mumbles, give a wave or just a nod to those with a room with a view

DELYTH:
- Winter's day - week day - Singleton Hospital chat about chemo
- Business-like meeting, the bottom line
- Café next to the small room, hear everyday going on outside
- Small room, 4 chairs, a table and a printer in the corner
- A4 white sheet of paper, grey lifeline
- 3% chance it would come back, 97% it would not on the case studies
- The discussion to have chemo was done on case studies, in my case 10,000 white women under 50.
- Sarah - lost 6 months earlier to chemo.
- Wasn't good enough
- No decision made, very distressed
- December meeting with Simon Holt, America
- Return before Christmas meeting - new treatment in the States – we would go for it
- Paid on his card - £1,800
- 26 sessions of radiotherapy and 3 breast surgeries

by then.
- Agreed my treatment plan, still do, business like
- Bob went to America, I never did

DELYTH:
- 15 weeks we waited, for the email to drop in from America
- Sunday morning in May, swimming , spring day
- Refreshing the laptop, the promise not to open
- Email in, opened
- Monday morning Simon Holt, another A4 white sheet of paper, results from America
- Based on my tumour, based on Bob, based on me
- It said what my reoccurrence rate was, far more active then they thought
- Chemo needed, TAC, Singleton Hospital Trial
- Hormonal treatment wouldn't work, ovaries had to be removed at the end of the chemo
- 27% chance it would come back, how wrong they had got it
- Now I looked ill and could no longer hide it
- 5 sessions of TAC, concerned they would kill me on 6th, isolation unit Singleton
- 5 years of trials, NICE have agreed it for the UK, for the testing process to be made available free to everyone under 50
- More recently to those under 70
- Tailored treatment plan, like I had
- I am case study A - Delyth Jones

STEPH: In 2016 I was 'bullied' by a friend to join her in the Tenovus Cancer Care Choir. I can't sing but was dragged along anyway. Since then I'd been sitting only feet from Delyth not knowing her story.

Then we both attended the storytelling workshop and, on that day, as we sat in a circle in that room of grey and glass with the black floor, I listened to Delyth and I realised that it was because of her I was being treated as an individual... When I was diagnosed with cancer and discussed it with my consultant I was offered a personal treatment plan which, back then, had only just been rolled out across the country.

I did not know how much Delyth had done for me and for thousands of others throughout the UK – men as well as women - for helping to pioneer this tailor-made approach.

So, thank you, Mr Holt, thank you, the American research team and, definitely, thank you, Delyth.............Because of you, I am still here.

DELYTH: We are both still here.

Belonging

What do you see when you stand before me?
A wobbly person, fat and framed?
Dare I believe that you are willing
To see more than just my frame?

I'm still here and I'm still living,
Come and sing and be profound.
Don't forget though – I have still got
The dirtiest laugh in town.

There is more to me than you
Can ever presume.
Adversity's not stopped me
Feeling joy and love to bloom.

I'm still here and I'm still living,
Come and sing and be profound.
Don't forget though – I have still got
The dirtiest laugh in town.

I dare you to be authentic.
Are you game to come and play?
Exploring in kind abundance
God's gift expressed – hooray!
I'm still here and I'm still living,
Come and sing and be profound.
Don't forget though – I have still got
The dirtiest laugh in town.

My Son

I had a son
who lives in China
a stranger to himself
no less than I am cancelled
murdered even
yet somewhere still in the space between us

I would sit on your doorstep
every day
for even a glimpse
if you did not live so far away

welcome to woman hood

"Talk less, smile more".

Although this is a line from *Hamilton*, this is told to girls around the world every day.

Be nice to customers and your reward is to be followed home.

We'll blame crimes on your outfit.

Call us out and we'll call you crazy.

Stay safe in this maze navigating the male gaze.

To every growing girl, my sisters you are strong.
You can dress how you want.

The ocean runs through your veins and my god will you make waves.

The Excuses We Make/ Patriarchal Excuse Generator

God made us this way
I wasn't myself
I lacked good male role models
I can't help it
It's just the way it's always been
I never made the problem
It never did my mother any harm
It wasn't that bad
You've never complained before
It wasn't my fault
She was asking for it

Egghead

Egghead is his name,
"Football is a boys' game"
He would never let girls play football,
Only rounders in the sports hall,
Wicked Witch of the West is her name,
"Netball is a girls' game"
She would never let the boys play netball
Only rugby in the sports hall.
Only game together is dodgeball
Stop being sexist this is our call

How do I teach my boys?

Treat others badly, that's truly your shame
Equal rights is acceptance that we're not all the same
Diversity is a dance and we've come a long way
But there are still differences in conditions and pay

Still differences in who can cry and who can't
Still politics involved in who can and can't make art
Still gaps in the system, progress is so start-stop-start
But in the mess of it all I hold hope in my heart

Medicine

New normals are not normals

—

Now I'm forty I drink my coffee with the fun removed.
Decaff, oatmilk, reheated.

—

Writing down these little thoughts on my phone, big
thoughts even, as they jump around my head. Memories,
memoirs, shopping lists, a never ending To Do.

Someone once told me it was poetry, the art of writing
down thoughts in the beautiful way in which your mind
created them, pictured them and told them to you.

I'm unconvinced by the beauty but calling it poetry
makes it seem more legitimate than the crazed ramblings
of a middle aged woman, so I shall name it.

—

Derestricted
I miss the regular messages asking if anyone needs
something from the shop, can you pick me up some milk,
bread, daren't hope for eggs, shall we split a wholesale
sack of flour between the 5 of us? I hear the corner shop
has yeast, corner shops are better stocked than Tesco's
right now. Doorstep surprise paper bags of coloured
card and tissue paper, patterns for a cut out doll, painted
rocks, a chocolate bar. Help yourself to books, puzzles

and DVDs we are bored of, they're out the front along with a bag of hand-me-down clothes for anyone who needs them. Charity shops and libraries are closed so we make our own.

———

Yesterday's Lunch rejected for an unforgivable crime. Soggy sandwiches.

And then I was her, sent home to our council house with free school meal of tuna in vinegar seeping through thin white sticky rounds.

She exchanged them for her own and ate them herself so that I wouldn't have to endure this Thatcher sanctioned ration.

'It's cheese but it's got mayo on it' she explains. And I am thankful for the option of wasting the meal.

———

I loved every last millimetre of my Nana. Especially her arms. Her all embracing bosom smothering large arms. I would like to love my own as much as I loved hers.

———

Imagining and creating truths forged like glass in the furnace of your soul. You share your universal truths beneath these words and worry you give too much away.

———

Cer di

Ym murmur ac ym mharabl
di-eiriau dy stori,
rhyngom bwriwyd yr angor sy'n ddeall
ac ni all neb na dim dan haul
ei chodi hi'n llwyr o'm llaw,
ac ni ddaw dydd traul i'w haearn tryloyw
na rhwd i'w rhaff;

ond mi wn,
gwn yn saff,
fel pob tad a mam,
y daw awr ei dirwyn,
am mai cariad yw dweud - 'cer di';

a rywfodd, bryd hynny,
pan fyddaf i'n gryfach,
a thithau'n ysu taith,
wele fi'n gadael fynd
heb adael fynd ychwaith.

Masiiwa the sheltered widow

She carries the calabash down the mountain to the creek
Bends her back under the cruel sun
Her eyes sun torched and back sun scorched
Her broken chipped feet
Swooshing and swashing in the narrow opening
Carries the calabash in up and down motions to and
from her tin
The weight lifetimes on her back
Ladens her shoulders with cares she cannot tell
A soul
She battles with twigs and sticks of the forest
As she
Labours to put a hot meal in the tummies
Of her 5 hungry babes
She scrapes the bottom of her pot
Willing more soup to come forth
To curb the hunger of her fatherless lot
They have names for her in the village
They call her
Masiiwa, asina muriritiri
The calluses on her hands extend into defined contours
As she labours for what will put
Miriro, Tamira, Vimbai, Matipa and Tariro through school
More or less feed them daily
Her troubles trouble sleep from her eyes
But invite waterfalls nightly, sobs drenched in prayers to
God

Most common words in anguish are
Mwari weshirikadzi nenherera
Muriritiri
Her pleas are for him to look upon her with mercy and
grace
Little does she know that he holds her hands so she
stands firm
Makes sure sickness and disease stay far from her
Each day he increases the desire in Tamira
To excel and be the best he can be
Teaches Miriro diligence and patience
Trains Matipa appreciation and love
Kindness and excellence the ribbons in Tariro's hair
Beacons of hope that keep her Fatherless lot smiling
each day they
See mama making it through one day at a time
Looking back Tamira sees the grace trail in how
Fees were paid without fail
Groceries enough to get them through week by week
Their prayers were answered not in the way they
expected them to be
But in the way they needed him to show through
Mwari weshirikadzi nenherera
Muriritiri, the father to the fatherless
Scholarships to Harvard didn't just happen in the back of
beyond
Nowhere in Chirumhanzi
Tamira smiles again as he sees her in his mind's eye
Reaching out to scavenge for hohwa and mowa
In the country region where he came from

His mother Masiiwa
Amai in all sense
He can see her now in that pale yellow dress
The sun had since discoloured
Masiiwa, a woman of courage and substance
A woman of virtue and honour
Who had shunned offers of easy come pleasures
Luxuries of dating after being widowed
To feed her hungry lot of 5
Had knelt down constantly, through all the bitter
The bad and the unlikely, remained steadfast
Remembering her nightly prayer
Mwari weshirikadzi nenherera
Muriritiri, the father to the fatherless
How she would bend her back but now no more
But to look at her sandaled feet
And wonder at her once chipped and marred feet
The weight of the world no longer the story of her life
Her once sun torched back and scorched eyes now know
The pleasures of shade and covering
Masiiwa who had trudged on stubbornly
Determined to argue with the present until it forged
A bright future for her 5
Now they have a new name for her in the village
They call her maduwe
Diaspora wavo
The lender to many and the borrower to none
Now her story is their story
They scratch each other's back to talk about Masiiwa
And how God heard her prayer and how he truly is

Mwari weshirikadzi nenherera
Ungati ndiye here starts the story of her life now
They forget the calloused hands and marred feet
A shame the stomach cannot give an account of how
Many times it rumbled in times past without food and
without fail
Now her battle is to make known how God came through
for her
The reason she will wear sandals but never relocate to
the suburbs
But would rather forage in the forest
Just to find labelled and cast away Masiiwas like herself
Strengthening them always with her usual line
Mwari weshirikadzi nenherera Muriritiri
The father to the fatherless.

Poams

When you were seven I said I was giving up;
you broke from your colouring to ask, *What?
Give up what, Mam?* Maybe your child's ear
needed assurance I did not mean you
(I hadn't realised I'd said it aloud). *Poems,
writing, trying to juggle all that, that's all.*

You laid your blue down, deliberate,
shifted the tone in your voice so you became
my mother that time, potato in palm,
peeler pointing at me, sorting those tears out.

*Well, you can't give up. You been doin them poams
since you was little, and look now, you got me
doin them too; and I'm brilliant!*
Your words were a hoof to my doubt.

You let the dust of the kick settle
then picked up your pencil and finished the sky
—some spilled from the page onto the table,
the wide sky, which you later filled
with birds and other winged creatures.

Mother-artist

They've got a problem with mother-artist it seems
They do not want it to go together
How could I tell you about my next-door neighbour
Who supplied ice-lollies all summer?

How could I tell you
About the pethau bychain of the plague?
About my best-buttie Hefin turned milk-man
Every other day without fail.

How could I tell you 'bout Julie's womb wisdom
And our laps of rage 'round Ponty Park?
How could I bless this new bridge -
This regenerational landmark.

How could I tell you about my mini-rebel Eva
Who I sing dime-dime-dime to down the phone?
How could I tell you about artist-mother
Who cooked up a new culture in her home?

How could I have built up huge resilience?
Mother-artist is my peaceful protest...
How could I show my daughters what to do?
Mother-artist is my prayer for progress...

My Grannies Were Witches

My grannies were witches

And my dad sprinted from one matriarchy

To another.

It's no wonder I turned out like this

When where I come from

Women rule.

Winnie the White cursed her husband

Her jailer

With urine from the chamber pot

As he sat in a drunken stupor

"It's raining!" he exclaimed.

She was turned away

From a women's refuge

Who thought a violent husband

Was a home.

He died abruptly

And when she was asked

How long he'd been dead

She said "Not long enough".

All folk said

She was canny

A witch.

My granny Marion

Left her very first baby

And sold her breastmilk

As if to say, the only one

Who profits off my commoditization

Is me.

She left this reality eventually.

Yelled incantations and curses down the phone

Saw and heard things

That nobody else could see

Thought medicine was poison

A belief which ended her life.

Why am I still so scared?

They say blood never lies

And I smile Winnie's smile

My spells and my blessings for

Mary, Marian, Marion

My spite and my rejection

Of what is expected of me

My life has become a conundrum

Of

Which

Witch?

Synopsis

Don Quixote is a 1605-1615 two-part book by Spaniard Miguel Cervantes about Don Quixote who goes insane binge-reading romantic chivalric tales of knights. Deluded he's a knight-errant, our hero dons makeshift armour and mounts his trusty past-prime nag Rociante to right wrongs, accompanied by dispairing friend Sancho Panza. Quixote's life is to defend the vulnerable against bullies and to do good deeds. Tilting his lance at windmills, convinced they are flailing four-armed evil giants. It didn't end well – so often doesn't against inanimate objects and apathy! His friends stage an intervention and tell him chivalry is dead yet he continues, unabated, on his adventures. After his final defeat, vanquished at the disguised hand of a duplicitous yet well-meaning friend, he withdraws to bed feverish and despondent telling Sancho chivalry really is dead. Yet Sancho suggests Quixote was right all along, Quixote doesn't accept this and dies.

- The End -

Conclusion

When you're swimming against the tide, a loving heart and blind faith can often be the noblest of traits. This prose is dedicated all us female Signorã Quixotã.

Titling At Windmills
(The Rise And Demise Of Signorã Quixotã)

The light's dropping, candle's dripping, eye's drooping;
you get the picture, it's getting way too late.
Insanely thumbing through page upon page,

can't put it down, just one more instalment, already at
chapter VIII.

Titling at windmills, epic fail!
The Enemy Enchanter's canvas sails appear, at first
glance, to have won.
Unflappably vanquishing evil or dying trying.
Never relinquishing righteousness
until the good fight's exhaustively fought, justice
eventually done.

Remount beloved Rociante,
valiant workhorse, warhorse, past-prime steadfast nag
'o'mine.
Splice splintered windmill-damaged lance,
readjust armour of distressed leather glued to hessian
sack
bang-out lacklustre, dented, riveted, rusty tin.
Double-down on determination to eradicate all of evil,
or else life's not worth living if you're just gonna let bad
people win.

It feels a lot like drowning, swimming constantly against
the tide.
Defending what's good, what's right, forcing evil to turn
and hide.

I still have 30 or so flailing-limbed canvas-sailed giants yet
to slay today.
For a quixotic knight-errant though,
when it comes to toppling towering tyrants,
NEVER is EVER too late in the day.

Long of tooth,
long gone her youth.
Defending what's pure in a world of deception,
a knight-errant must unswervingly serve upholding her
truth.

Thin of skin, yet thick of head,
know thine enemy Signorã Quixotã;
charlatans, imposters, false prophets, Ephraimite
bowmen who stole cattle and played false in the day of
battle,
just one word for them... shibboleth.
Old Quixotã here won't stop until either the world's put
to rights,
or she draws her last living breath.

It feels a lot like drowning, swimming constantly against
the tide.
Defending what's good, what's right, forcing evil to turn
and hide.

So watch out all doers of evil in all it's nefarious forms,
in all it's nine circles of hell:
the pagan, perve, glutton; the grabby, rageful, heretic;
the violent, fraud and treacherous traitor;
Cain, Antenora, Ptolemy, Judas Iscariot with a fistfull of
silver pieces as well.

Then in heaven, a war broke out.
Michael and his two third legion of angels fought the
great dragon,
who was hurled to Earth in the affray.

The serpent devil with his one third angels,
heaven sent whilst hell bent on leading this imperfect
world astray.

And so as the ass saw the angel,
Ballam finally understood and bowed down his humbled
head.
Babel's tower toppled, Babylon burned,
the winged woman wrapped in the sun, into the
wilderness, under God's protection, from the evil great
dragon, fled.

Befuddled, bemused, bewildered, confused,
unflappable, unstoppable, tragic, absurd and nothing left
to lose.
Aspirational, delusional, ridiculed, sincere,
misunderstood,
yet 'tis more nobler to die trying than to compromise
even an inch,
in the fight against evil for what's pure, altruistic and
good.

For Siniorã Quixotã though, it didn't end well.
So I guess I'll either see you in a jail,
or in an institution,
or for sure, eternally, in hell.

For all us Signorã Quixotãs,
it's difficult to know where, or even if, to draw the line.
All or nothing, life or death, black or white,
splitting good from evil, boundaried and borderlined.
It feels a lot like drowning, swimming constantly against

the tide.
Defending what's good, what's right, forcing evil to turn and hide.

Beaten and battered and forsworn of her chivalrous truths.
Battle weary, spent, conflicted, depleted and deflated by strife.
She feverishly, fearlessly slipped the shackles,
of her tortured, moral, mortal life.

And in that final hour of the seventh day, peace descended,
nature's harmonics converged as her stars aligned.
Enveloped by, drawn toward, Haniel's orgastic turquoise-green light.
Goodnight sweetheart, defender, champion caballera.
Goodnight sweetest, noblest, misguided, kind-of-heart, errant-knight.

It must have felt a lot like she was drowning,
As Siniorã Quixotã swam constantly against the tide.
Defending what's good and right, she forced evil to turn and hide.

In conclusion dearest patient reader,
if Signorã Quixotã's plight, in any way, to you relates,
when it feels as if the Enemy Enchanter's windmills are winning,
be assured that a loving heart and blind faith are the noblest of traits.

a good mother

when my daughter was four years old

and behaving well

i let her pick a toy

from the shop on the high street

i think it was a mouse she chose

or maybe a rat

anyway it was pink and soft and fluffy

and she treated it like it was real

she called her baby

baby.

she was a good mother.

she fed it with her plastic spoons

the ones i had used to feed her

the summer before last

but proud and big now she used the metal ones

all by herself.

she tucked her baby in at night

and slept with it

and in the mornings she would take it to school

she couldn't bear to be without her baby

all day long

but one morning when we got to the gates

we realised baby was gone

it had fallen out somewhere along the way

slipped through buttons and fabric

the tears went down her cheeks

i had never seen her cry like that

her screams startled the other mothers in the playground

she didn't want to go to school

but i promised i'd find her baby

it would be on a windowsill

found by someone and safely left

or face down in a puddle

but then i would take it home

and dry it off on the radiator.

my legs hurt

but i retraced our route a hundred times

because i knew how she felt

or at least

i could imagine what it would be like

to lose her

it was no-where though

so i replaced her baby

with the exact same one from the high street shop

the same colour

and everything

but somehow

like any good mother

she knew.

she did not want to feed the substitute

with her plastic spoons

she left it to starve up on her bedroom shelf

next to the etch a sketch

and the cabbage patch doll

unwanted christmas and birthday gifts

she would not let me tuck her in that night

or kiss her

she turned her wet cheek to the pillow

and i cried

because i was sorry i could not find her baby

i thought maybe if i did

for once i would feel like a good mother

too.

Gwladys Ellen

Gwelaf di, Gwladys Ellen – ddynes gref;
trwy lygaid heddiw, dwi'n gwerthfawrogi,
gwarchodwr caredig cleifion pentref.

Yn fy nghof rwyt yn adlais o gartref,
er ges di fyth y cylchgrawn-hyfryd-dŷ;
gwelaf di, Gwladys Ellen – ddynes gref.

Holl henoed yr ardal – dy haid â'u bref,
canys ti oedd 'fengaf yn dy deulu;
gwarchodwr caredig cleifion pentref.

Prydferth trwy dy einioes, hyd dy hydref,
er ges di fyth cyfle i briodi;
gwelaf di, Gwladys Ellen – ddynes gref.

Tynged y merthyr, wnes di ddioddef;
a'th freuddwydion dy hun, wnes di gelu.
Ond, welaf di Gwladys Ellen, ddynes gref,
gwarchodwr caredig cleifion pentref.

Gwladys Ellen

I see you, Gwladys Ellen – strong woman,
through today's eyes, I appreciate,
kind custodian of the village's unwell.

In my mind you are an echo of home,
although you never had the magazine-lovely-house,
I see you, Gwladys Ellen – strong woman.

The elderly of the area, were your flock with their
breying,
because you were the youngest in your family.
kind custodian of the village's unwell.

Beautiful through your lifetime, and your autumn,
although you never had the chance to marry;
I see you, Gwladys Ellen – strong woman.

Fate of the martyr, you suffered,
and your own dreams, you concealed.
I see you, Gwladys Ellen – strong woman,
kind custodian of the village's unwell.

In the Name of the Female Gender

Echo stripped off
her ethereal existence
Daphne her foliage
and Chloe quivered
the dew from her hair

they armed themselves with
bravery, courage and power
to swoop in silently
all together
on to the centaur
to defend themselves
in the depths
of time and place
in the name of all
wronged women
to win the blood back
to create justice
in the name
of the female gender

Wonderland Everywhere

We see madness in everyone we meet,
we drink tea every now and then whilst playing cards,
and we see cats who stay for one second
and leave our sight the next.
You don't need a rabbit to guide you,
for every day is a day in Wonderland.

Birds Still Sing in my Garden

The hot sun hits my face.
So what if it's not normal to sit in a cemetery eating
chips.
I took normal for granted for an eternity.
Forever narrowing down the choices,
Putting up fences.
Guarded, groping, grasping, grappling with my
conscience.
Guided by what was correct.
I look back to see how far I've come.
I am standing still.
But birds still sing in my garden.
Discarding the serious, I join them.
I am no longer depressed
And I sing, sing, sing.

The Art of Sitting in Circle

Sitting in circle with other mothers
is getting advice on your stubborn child
to brush their teeth -
"tell them black bugs will come live in their mouth".

Sitting in circle with other mothers
is bad-mouthing without judgement
is cursing annoying toys
"especially the chicken from the childless co-worker".

Sitting in circle we become one
and celebrate self for seeing things through.
This is the hardest job ever, no two ways work,
but we all absolutely definitely hate Lego.